FaithBuilders #9—
Why Go to Church?

FaithBuilders #9— Why Go to Church?

. . . and Other Bible Lessons for Kids

C. W. Bess and Roy E. DeBrand

Baker Books

A Division of Baker Book House Co
Grand Rapids, Michigan 49516

© 1985 by C. W. Bess and Roy E. DeBrand

Published by Baker Books
a division of Baker Book House Company
P.O. Box 6287, Grand Rapids, MI 49516-6287

New paperback edition published 2001

Previously published as *Bible-Centered Object Sermons for Children*

Printed in the United States of America

ISBN 0-8010-6373-6

Unless otherwise indicated, Scripture quotations are from the Revised Standard Version of the Bible, copyright 1946, 1952, 1971 by the Division of Christian Education of the National Council of the Churches of Christ in the USA. Used by permission.

Scripture quotations identified KJV are from the King James Version of the Bible.

Scripture quotations identified LB are from *The Living Bible* © 1971. Used by permission of Tyndale House Publishers, Inc., Wheaton, IL 60189. All rights reserved.

Scripture quotations identified NIV are from the HOLY BIBLE, NEW INTERNATIONAL VERSION®. NIV®. Copyright © 1973, 1978, 1984 by International Bible Society. Used by permission of Zondervan Publishing House. All rights reserved.

Scripture quotations identified NKJV are from the New King James Version. Copyright © 1979, 1980, 1982 by Thomas Nelson, Inc. Used by permission. All rights reserved.

Scripture quotations identified TEV are from the Good News Bible, Today's English Version. Copyright © American Bible Society 1966, 1971, 1976. Used by permission.

For current information about all releases from Baker Book House, visit our web site:

http://www.bakerbooks.com

Contents

1

All Things New

Interest Object: One peanut in original shell.

Main Truth: Ours is an exciting world where God makes everything new.

Scripture Text: "Behold, I make all things new" (Rev. 21:5).

Do you like a riddle or mystery? Try to guess what I hold in my hand. I promise that you have never seen this particular object before. In fact, no one else has ever viewed it either. It has always been in the dark and has never seen the light of day.

Perhaps I should wait a few moments for you to think. This is one of a kind! You will be very surprised. Now the suspense is building.

No, it is not a beam of light or some exotic invention. This is something very common but one which you have never seen before.

Let me add to the mystery. You will see it for only a minute. Then it will disappear forever. You will be the first to see it, and then it will never be seen again. Gone forever.

Are you ready to see something never seen before and never to be seen again? [At this point open your hand to reveal a peanut shell. Open the shell, and show a peanut.]

You say you have seen a peanut before? Oh, but you have not seen this particular peanut. And you will never see it again. Watch it disappear forever when I swallow it!

Were you disappointed? Yes, I did play a trick on you. Most riddles are so simple they fool us. But I wanted to explain how everything God makes is an original creation.

You had seen many peanuts before, but not that one peanut. It was just made fresh and new by God. But that is not all God makes. He is still in the business of making people new, also. "Behold, I make all things new."

2

Open Up

Interest Object: A camera and some dark pictures.

Main Truth: Open your life and let in the light of Jesus.

Scripture Text: "You are to open their eyes and turn them from the darkness to the light, and from the power of Satan to God . . ." (Acts 26:18, TEV).

Here is a new camera with the best features to take pretty pictures, but look at these snapshots. They are so dark we can't see anything!

What happened? A camera needs the exact amount of light coming in through the lens. Think of this glass lens as a window which I can make larger to let in more light on a cloudy day. Or if there is too much sunlight, I can turn the dial making the window smaller.

Isn't that what you do for good pictures with your two cameras? You shake your heads to say that you don't own two cameras? Yes, you do. I can see those cameras right on your face.

Your eyes are like cameras. You must open them to have enough light to see. When you go into a dark theater, your eyes need more light, so the pupil inside gets bigger to let in more light. Then when you come out of the dark theater into the bright light, the opposite happens. You have too much light, so you squint and your pupils become smaller.

Long ago Saul didn't like Jesus Christ or anyone who followed the Lord. Saul had authority to arrest all of God's people he could find and put them in prison. He was on his way to a foreign city called Damascus looking for Christians who loved Jesus. Every Christian he saw would be put in prison.

About noon a light much brighter than the sun caused Saul to squint his eyes and fall fearfully down in the dust. His eyes were blinded!

Then Jesus spoke. Saul must stop doing bad things and start helping foreigners who lived in darkness. When God gave Saul's sight back, he became a preacher known by his other name, Paul.

In his sermons Paul loved to tell how Jesus said: "You are to open their eyes and turn them from the darkness to the light and from the power of Satan to God, so that through their faith in me they will have their sins forgiven and will receive their place among God's chosen people."

Open up! That is the idea. Our lives are like a camera or like your two eyes. We must turn from the darkness to the light. Living without God is like living in darkness with Satan. Open your eyes and turn toward the light which is Jesus.

3

The Speck

Interest Object: Open picture frame and two towels.

Main Truth: Recognize your own sins instead of pointing to the sins of others.

Scripture Text: "Why do you see the speck that is in your brother's eye, but you do not notice the log that is in your own eye?" (Matt. 7:3).

Today we are going to wash a window. Because we don't want any broken glass, just pretend that this picture frame is a window with glass inside. Here are two towels which are real, however. Now I will pick two of you to pretend you are washing the window.

One is on the outside and the other is the inside. Each of you is responsible for your own side, so clean all the spots from your side.

But everyone knows what happens now. After you get your side clean, you see through the pane of glass

11

and notice lots of spots on your partner's side. You knock on the glass and point to his spot. "Clean that dirty spot on your side of the window!"

"That's not my spot. It is your spot. Clean it yourself," your partner says.

So you give your side another swipe, but the blemish does not disappear. Now you know for sure it's not your fault. When your partner refuses to accept blame, you decide to walk outside and say, "Look, I'll wipe your spot off. That will prove you are blind!"

Oops! It looks different from the other side. You realize that the spot was in your eye, not on the window.

How easy to find fault in others without seeing something worse in our own lives. In His Sermon on the Mount, Jesus warned us about this very thing.

How ridiculous for me to say, "I see you have a big speck in your eye. You ought to do something about it." But at the same time I have a big log sticking out of my eye. That would be silly, wouldn't it?

When it comes to finding fault, we need look no further than our own selves. So don't worry so much about the sins of others. Notice your own sins instead.

4

An Apple a Day

Interest Object: An apple.

Main Truth: Don't miss the good parts of worship.

Scripture Text: ". . . refresh me with apples; for I am sick with love" (Song of Sol. 2:5).

$\mathbf{A}$n apple a day keeps the doctor away." That is an old saying which describes how nutritious an apple is to the body. Eating an apple each day helps us stay strong and healthy. If we are not sick, then the doctor stays away from us.

A curious verse found in Song of Solomon mentions an apple and sickness. It is not about regular sickness or fever but a delightful sickness called love. Some people say that falling in love is much like being sick.

This verse comes from the love poems which King Solomon and his lover wrote to each other. Of course, you know about love notes. In a few years you might be writing these notes to someone you like in school. King Solomon's lover wrote these words to him:

"Refresh me with apples; for I am sick with love." What an unusual way of recognizing that an apple a day keeps the doctor away! She wanted Solomon to bring her an apple. That way she could see him and feel better.

That is all we know about Solomon and apples. But we are certain that apples are very nutritious and can make us feel good. They contain vitamins, minerals and food value excellent for the body.

The most nutritious portion of an apple is the first part. You may call it the outside part or the peel. If you take a knife and remove the peel, then you start eating too late. Some of the best vitamins are in this apple skin.

Then most of us quit eating the apple too soon. We throw away the last part which is the core. Did you know that an apple core is very good for you? Don't worry about the seeds. They are an excellent source of fiber for the digestive system.

But how does this relate to children in church today? Well, we come to church to keep spiritually healthy. Reading the Bible, singing, praying and listening to the pastor's sermon are like food for your soul. Worship in church helps keep you spiritually strong instead of sick.

Yet many people miss some of the best parts of worship. Like those who peel the skin from an apple, they come late and miss the beginning. They miss the quiet prayer time prior to worship.

Other people want to throw away the last part. They act uninterested in the altar call, the decisions publicly shared, or the benediction and the wonderful time of fellowship as members are leaving.

They are thinking about the wrong kind of food. "I

wish everything would end so we can get to a restaurant and be first in line." Or, "I hope my roast does not burn at home."

So worship is like an apple. Don't miss the first part or the last part. Come early and stay late!

5

Be Filled

Interest Object: Soft plastic bottle.

Main Truth: Keep your hearts and minds filled with good thoughts.

Scripture Text: "And God's peace, which is far beyond human understanding, will keep your hearts and minds safe in union with Christ Jesus. In conclusion, my brothers, fill your minds with those things that are good and deserve praise: things that are true, noble, right, pure, lovely and honorable" (Phil. 4:7–8, TEV).

Here is a clear plastic bottle which appears to be empty. I hold the container upside down with the lid removed. If any liquid had been inside before, we know that it would have flowed out by now.

Can we say, therefore, that this bottle is completely empty? Be careful now! That is a tricky question.

Yes, the bottle is empty of soap, soup, sand, or soda

pop. But something clear and invisible is still inside the bottle. Can you guess what it is? That is right. The bottle is full of air.

By holding the bottle to your ear and quickly squeezing it, you can hear the sound of air being forced out. When I release my strong grip, the bottle springs back into its original shape and draws air back inside.

Scientists tell us that nothing on earth is ever empty in its natural form. Water, sand, or air will always rush in to fill every shell, ball, or cup.

You may be very hungry and feel empty inside. Perhaps you foolishly skipped breakfast and now your stomach feels empty. It isn't completely empty. Your hunger pangs come from the stomach which squeezes itself into a little ball around a little air and digestive juice.

Our hearts and minds are similar. We always have some thoughts or memories inside. We are never empty, but will always be filled with some thoughts or ideas. For the most part, we have a choice in how our hearts and minds will be filled.

Some people are always thinking bad thoughts about others. Jesus once described some religious leaders as being "like whitewashed tombs, which outwardly appear beautiful, but within they are full of dead men's bones and all uncleanness" (Matt. 23:27).

Instead of thinking bad thoughts about others, we ought to fill our minds with good thoughts. God helps us keep our hearts and minds safe in Christ Jesus, but we must do our part, too. That is what the apostle Paul meant by saying "fill your minds with those things that are good and deserve praise: things that are true, right, pure, lovely and honorable."

6

Let It Shine

Interest Object: A table lamp, a flashlight, and a night-light.

Main Truth: Just be yourself while not worrying about others.

Scripture Text: "You are the light of the world. . . . Let your light so shine before men, that they may see your good works and give glory to your Father who is in heaven" (Matt. 5:14, 16).

Where would we be without the many kinds of lights in our homes? The answer to that question is obvious. We would be in the dark!

Consider these three sources of light which you probably have in your home. Here is a table lamp able to illuminate an entire room. This kind of light is necessary for reading your Bible or sewing a button on your clothes.

A night light is small and insignificant in the day. Compared to the table lamp, it is too dim to be noticed.

18

Oh, but how important is a little light at night when you get up for a trip to the bathroom. You would not want to stumble on a chair in the dark.

A flashlight is useful when the electricity is out. In an emergency we reach for this battery-powered light. It is also helpful to find small objects lost behind furniture or to catch nightcrawlers at dusk.

Each light is very different. What would happen if these three lights started arguing among themselves? The table lamp says, "I am most important because I give more light."

The night light replies, "Yes, but you are very expensive. Your bulbs burn out often and must be replaced. I am more important because in the dark I keep children from being afraid."

The flashlight boasts, "You are both wrong. In a real emergency I am most important. Besides, I can go anywhere in the house or outside. I am better than any other light."

After the argument each light is sorry. The lamp thinks, "They are right. My bulbs do not last very long. And I am expensive. I wish I were some other type of light."

Then the night light thinks, "I have so little to boast about. I'm embarrassed to be so small. People think of me as useful only to children. I wish I were as important as the other lights."

Wait a minute! What is happening here? These lights are forgetting that every light is unique. Each is important and has its own purpose. Lights are just like people.

Jesus said, "You are the light of the world." That makes us all very important. All light is good. We should be proud to let our light shine before people. Jesus meant that our light should be something good.

Jesus did not say: "Only the brightest of you can shine for me." He did not mean, "Only one type of light can shine for me." Every light is included.

You are a light for Jesus. Don't be jealous of other people who may seem to be a bigger or better or stronger light for Jesus. And don't feel sorry for yourself because you think your light is too small. God loves you just the way He made you. So shine, light, shine!

7

A Love Reflector

Interest Object: Red reflector glass.

Main Truth: God is our source of love.

Scripture Text: "We love, because he first loved us" (1 John 4:19).

Here is something very important for a bicycle or an automobile. It does not make a bicycle easier to peddle or make an automobile go faster. During the day this piece of red glass is useless, but it can save your life at night. Do you know what it is?

We call it a safety reflector or reflector glass. Unlike a flashlight or a headlight, it is not a light source. Yet this glass can reflect light so your bicycle can be seen at night.

One afternoon you might be so busy at a friend's home that you don't realize darkness is descending. Oh, my, you will be late! Then you jump on your bike and start peddling fast toward home. How dangerous! It is far better to telephone home and explain, than risk riding at night.

Because cars travel so much faster than bicycles, they can quickly overtake a child on a bicycle. Before the driver even sees you, it could be too late to stop. Then there might be a tragic accident.

That's how a reflector glass on the back of your bicycle could save your life. It reflects the headlights of a car so the driver can see you sooner. Then he can avoid the collision.

Even if you are not on the road at night, this reflector could save your bicycle. Sometimes you forget and leave your bicycle in the driveway at night. Then someone drives a car into your driveway and CRUNCH! That could happen if there is not a reflector light to send a warning.

And where does this glass get its light? Remember that it has no source of light in itself. But then a reflector doesn't need its own light because reflector glass shines back the light sent to it. The more it gets, the more it shines back.

This reminds us of God's love shining in our lives. We have no original love within us, but God sends His love to us which we reflect to other people. "We love, because He first loved us."

8

Right and Wrong Always

Interest Object: Popcorn sack or other litter object.

Main Truth: There are no exceptions to right or wrong.

Scripture Text: "Teach me, O Lord, the way of thy statutes; and I will keep it to the end" (Ps. 119:33).

Put yourself in this story. You are strolling down the street eating from a bag of popcorn. You reach the bottom of the sack and there is no more popcorn. So without thinking you carelessly wad the sack in a little ball and toss it on the ground.

Then a policeman calls you from behind, "Just a moment there! You broke the law." Oh, my! Where did he come from?

You turn around slowly with a guilty look on your face. A big policeman in a bright blue uniform stands there holding your crushed sack in his hand. You feel terrible.

"Don't you know that we have laws against littering?" he asks. "I ought to arrest you for breaking the law."

You say, "I am so sorry. I did not know. I just did not think. I will never do it again."

Then the policeman smiles a little and says: "Well, I suppose you could be let off this time with just a warning. I hope you have learned a lesson."

You reply, "Thank you, sir. You have taught me the right way to act, so I won't break this law again. I will keep it as long as I live."

So the policeman gives you back your sack, and you walk off greatly relieved. But then you wonder. What am I to do with this sack? There is no trashcan around, and I don't want to carry a greasy old bag all day.

You look around. Now the policeman is gone. You could get by with throwing the litter away again. It would be safe. But would it be right?

Long ago the psalmist loved God's law. He prayed that God would teach him right so he could do right. Not just when it was convenient to do right. But always, as long as he lived.

Right is always right. Wrong is always wrong. No exceptions. Once we are taught something is wrong, we should never do it. Not even if we are certain no policeman is close. Not even if we think God will let us off free. When we learn God's rules, we keep them always.

9

The Taste Test

Interest Object: Any fruit such as apple or banana.

Main Truth: The only way to find out if God is real is to try Him.

Scripture Text: "O taste and see that the Lord is good!" (Ps. 34:8).

Look what someone gave me. What a beautiful and delicious looking apple. Someone must love me very much to send this gift. But I wonder if this is a real apple. How can I tell if it is genuine?

It looks so juicy. I have never seen a prettier red apple. This fruit feels just right—not too hard and not too soft. It also smells like an apple. But how can I be sure that this is real?

You know the answer. It is a taste test. I can be sure only when my tongue and tummy tell me the truth. I must taste, chew, and swallow a bite of the apple.

It is the same with God. The psalmist said, "O taste and see that the Lord is good."

Of course, we can not really eat God. But we can trust God and love Him. We can feel His love just as we feel a warm sunbeam on our face.

But we can't taste an apple we can't reach or feel a sunbeam in the dark. To experience the great love of God, we cannot ignore or draw back from the taste test.

We must try or experience God's best gift to us which is simply God Himself. He has given Himself to us, and we must accept that love personally. "O taste and see that the Lord is good!"

10

Death as a Door

Interest Object: Picture of a tombstone.

Main Truth: Death is a doorway to heaven where Jesus waits for us.

Scripture Text: "Let not your hearts be troubled; believe in God, believe also in me. In my Father's house are many rooms; if it were not so, would I have told you that I go to prepare a place for you? And when I go and prepare a place for you, I will come again and will take you to myself, that where I am you may be also" (John 14:1–3).

This is a picture of a tombstone or a grave-marker. It is a sad sight when it reminds us of loved ones who have died. A graveyard or a tombstone might even cause us to be afraid of dying.

One night a mother and father heard the sound of sobbing in their son's bedroom. Little Billy was scared and crying in the dark. So the father got up and went into his son's bedroom to give him a good strong hug. Then he asked, "What is wrong, Billy?"

"I'm afraid," he replied.

"Does it have to do with your grandfather's death?" his father asked.

"Yes, I'm afraid I will die like grandfather."

"Son, we must all die someday. If you are afraid, let's talk about it. Perhaps it is because you do not understand what death really is. Death is simply a doorway to something better."

"A doorway to where, Dad?"

"To heaven. On the night before Jesus died, He promised to go prepare a better place for us. But not on earth. You know where?"

"Of course! Jesus meant heaven! But I don't want to go to heaven yet. I would rather stay here. I am afraid to leave."

"Billy, I'm sure that God will leave you here until you are grown up and have children of your own. But you don't need to be afraid of death. It is very much like being born. Of course, you were too small to remember that, but I remember very well. You must have thought it was hard to be born. You waited and waited. Then you finally came crying and screaming."

"You mean I was afraid of being born? Why?"

"It was because you did not know about the better place we had prepared for you. All you knew was the warm, dark place inside your mother's body where you were happy. But then the door opened, and you had to come out. I believe you were surprised how much better your new life was.

"The best part was that we were all waiting for you. We had loved you before you were ever born. Your mother and I and your grandfather, too.

28

"Now your grandfather is waiting again. He is in heaven, the perfect place prepared by Jesus for you, me and everyone who believes in Jesus.

"Just think of death as a doorway that leads to a better life in a prepared place called heaven. It must be good over there because Jesus has prepared everything just right."

Then before the father returned to his bed, he read some wonderful verses from John 14. We can read these same verses which tell us about this prepared place.

11

Whose Are You?

Interest Object: Covered bird cage with toy cat inside.

Main Truth: Where we are or who we are is not as important as whose we are.

Scripture Text: "So then, whether we live or whether we die, we are the Lord's" (Rom. 14:8).

Today I hold a covered bird cage with a little pet inside. In a little while I will introduce my pet named Tweetie, but first this question. What makes a person a Christian? Some people think that if you just go to church, then you are a Christian. But that is not always true.

Now before I go further, do you want to see my pet? Then I will remove the cover. [At this point all the children are quick to point to the absurd sight of the big stuffed cat in a bird cage. They shout, "That's no bird!"]

So you think this is not a bird. Is this not a bird cage?

And people put birds in bird cages. Therefore, this just must be a bird.

Of course, you are right. This silly cat is not a bird, even if he is inside a bird cage. It takes more than being in a bird cage to be a bird.

Who you are does not depend on *where* you are. You can be born in a garage, but that doesn't make you a car. You can sleep in a barn, but that does not mean you are a cow.

But most of all, you can be raised in church. You can come to church every week of your life, and that still does not automatically make you a Christian.

What is a Christian? A Christian is someone who simply believes in Jesus, who has asked Jesus to live inside his or her heart. You can invite Jesus into your heart while you are at home, at school or here at church. Where, makes no difference.

The important difference is not *where* we are or even *who* we are but *whose* we are. To be a Christian we must belong to Jesus.

> Now I belong to Jesus,
> Jesus belongs to me,
> Not for the years of time alone,
> But for eternity.

When we belong to Jesus, we belong to Him forever. It makes no difference where we may be. "Whether we live or die, then, we belong to the Lord."

12

Long-Distance Prayer

Interest Object: Picture of a telephone.

Main Truth: Distance does not matter in prayer.

Scripture Text: "The Lord hears when I call to him" (Ps. 4:3).

By now you know the difference between talking locally on a telephone and talking long distance. When we call someone in our own town or neighborhood, we don't worry about cost. When talking long distance, however, we hurry because the telephone call can become expensive. The farther the distance and the longer the time, the more expensive our conversation.

A long-distance telephone call used to be an exciting event which required the help of an operator. Friends and neighbors crowded close to the phone. Lots of static and background noises made it confusing. The voice on the other end sounded far away, so people would shout loudly into the phone. Often they could not hear.

Back then a long-distance call anywhere was just a few miles away. Now in some cities you can call many miles away and still have a local connection.

Today you can call across the ocean with ease. No operator is needed, and the sound is great. You can talk in a normal voice.

That is how prayer unto God is supposed to be. Distance doesn't matter. When we want to talk to God, we simply pray. There's no problem with bad connections or cost. No operator or priest is needed.

About the only problem we have with telephones is busy lines. Everyone wants to talk at once, so we hear a busy signal. Or we have to wait until a family member finishes with the phone so we can use it. That makes us wonder if God is ever too busy to hear us.

King David knew better. He understood that God is never too busy or too far away to hear us. David prayed often enough to be sure of that. Listen to his testimony: "The Lord hears when I call on him."

13

Look Up and Shine

Interest Object: A sunflower, either plastic or real.

Main Truth: Love God, look to Him and shine!

Scripture Text: "When Moses came down from Mount Sinai, with the two tables of the testimony in his hand as he came down from the mountain, Moses did not know that the skin of his face shone because he had been talking with God" (Exod. 34:29).

Do you like my flower? This popular flower grows in many countries. Even if you had never seen one before in your life, you could still guess its name.

This is not a moonflower. Neither is it a starflower. Can you guess now? This is a sunflower, a plant which does so much more than just look pretty.

Sunflowers grow anywhere the sun shines hot and bright. They protect land from erosion and produce seeds which are sold as feed for birds, chickens, and cattle. Sunflower seeds are also good for us to eat.

The sunflower follows its true love all day long. When the sun rises in the east, the sunflower leans in that direction. Then as the sun crosses the sky on its westward course, the sunflower follows it by tilting toward the light. By sunset the flower faces west, faithfully gathering the last warm rays of its beloved sun.

Unlike other flowers that are hard to pronounce or describe, the simple sunflower has a name easy to remember. And how appropriate is its name! Here is a flower which loves the sun so much that it even looks like the sun.

The Bible tells us that God is light. A long time ago Moses climbed a mountain called Sinai where he visited with our God of Light. Moses was up there many days. Finally he came down the mountain carrying stone tablets on which were engraved the Ten Commandments.

Moses did not know it, but his face was shining with the radiance of God. Like the sunflower, Moses began to look like the One he loved. He was bright like God.

In some ways we can be like God. A bright smile and face lit with enthusiasm can be a reflection of God's light. But first, we must love God and always look to Him.

14

You Are Valuable

Interest Object: Old diary or small ledger.

Main Truth: You are valuable.

Scripture Text: "But God shows his love for us in that while we were yet sinners Christ died for us" (Rom. 5:8).

Pretend that I am going to sell this old book which I found in my grandfather's attic. It appears to be a diary with lots of empty pages. What could it be worth?

Someone might suggest, "How much did it originally cost?" When we carefully examine the cover, we notice a faint mark. It says two cents. So that is the original price.

But it is old and used. Someone has already written on it, so we might suggest a price of one-half the original cost. That would equal one penny.

But wait! This book is so old that some people might consider it an antique. One of a kind. Very valuable. It would then be worth 100 dollars.

More good news! When we examine the writing in this diary, we recognize a famous name. This diary belonged to President Abraham Lincoln. That makes it very valuable indeed. Some people might pay $10,000 for a historical treasure.

Isn't this exciting? Somebody calls me up to say, "I am a writer. I can take your diary and write a book and perhaps a documentary for television. It might even be made into a movie. I will pay one million dollars for your book!"

What a fun-filled fantasy! Our little game demonstrates how the world determines value. Something that looks worthless can be very valuable.

Crowded around me are lots of children. Are you very valuable? That depends on how we measure your value.

Your body is composed of chemicals and basic substances which could be sold for two or three dollars. Or you could sell a quart of your blood for even more. But surely you are worth more alive than dead!

Are you rare, only one of a kind? Look around. Millions of boys and girls just like you live all over the world. You are as common as weeds in a garden. Some people say there are too many children today and not enough food. The more boys and girls in the world, the less valuable they are.

Your value might also depend on whether you are good or bad. Will you always obey? In some countries they sell boys and girls as slaves. No one wants to buy a child who will not obey.

These are some of the ways the world might determine your value, but they are all the wrong ways. The Bible teaches that you are very precious. God made you. And He loves you. He loved you before you were ever born. Even when you do bad things, God still loves you.

In Romans 5:8 we learn how much God really loves us all. "But God shows his love for us in that while we were yet sinners Christ died for us."

Think of that! Jesus didn't wait until we became good enough to love us. He loved us as we are—enough to pay the greatest price possible to save us. Jesus has already died to show His love and prove how valuable we are to Him, even though we continue to do wrong things.

15

Little Children and Big Rockets

Interest Object: A toy rocket or picture of a space rocket.

Main Truth: Little children are important.

Scripture Text: "Let the children come to me, and do not hinder them; for to such belongs the kingdom of heaven" (Matt. 19:14).

A rocket launch is exciting to watch. There is such a thunderous sound when the fuel ignites! What power is in that explosion! Stand back! We should not be too close in case anything goes wrong and the entire ship explodes. For that reason we have to keep a safe distance.

You may wonder. How do they start the rocket launch? Not with a match. They do it by remote control.

In the early days of our American rocket program,

our rockets were very simple. A giant pipe was filled with fuel and ignited by a heavy battery. But how did the battery know when to send its spark?

A transmitting device sent the GO signal to the battery which started the rocket with a big spark. When the button was pushed, the first stage of the rocket ignited, and the rocket was lifted up high into the air. Then another push of the button would ignite the second stage of the rocket to carry it much higher.

Everyone was ready on the day of a very important rocket launch. The button was pushed, the spark released and the big rocket lifted off. What a thrilling sight! A few moments later they pushed the button for the second stage. But this time nothing happened! Having used only half its fuel, the big rocket fell back toward the earth and was destroyed.

What was the problem? Not with the rocket. Not in the fuel. The trouble was in the transmitter which would not send a signal because its little battery had quit working. Imagine that! A big rocket ship costing millions of dollars was destroyed because a ten-cent battery was not working.

Maybe the small battery was tired of being neglected or felt that his place was not important. Or he may have been sleeping on the job. Oh, but the little battery was just as important as the big rocket ship.

One time some children were brought to Jesus that He might put His hands on them and pray. The disciples around Jesus had many important things to do. They did not want Jesus being bothered by little people. Then Jesus saw what was happening. He told the disciples they were wrong. The little children were just as important as the big people.

Listen to what He said about children just like you. "Let the children come to me, and do not hinder them; for to such belongs the kingdom of heaven."

16

Strength in Him

Interest Object: A large magnet, a small magnet, and a handful of metal paper clips.

Main Truth: We can do more with Jesus' strength added to our own.

Scripture Text: "I can do all things in him who strengthens me" (Phil. 4:13).

Magnets make useful tools and fun toys. Today we can use this big magnet, this small magnet, and a handful of paper clips to learn a valuable lesson about letting God help us. The larger magnet represents big people, but we will lay it aside for a moment.

Now pretend you are a little magnet. You can't do big jobs like grownups, but you still have responsibilities and tasks your own size. Like obeying parents. And brushing your teeth.

Each of these important tasks can be represented by a

paper clip. I am attaching a couple of paper clips for obeying parents and brushing your teeth. They make a chain. You can add to this chain by naming other chores like picking up your clothes off the floor.

Soon the little magnet can hold no more. When we try to add more paper clips, they all fall off.

At this point you say, "I can't do any more. I need more strength." And so you do.

Then along comes this bigger magnet which represents Jesus. He offers His strength to help us do many things too hard for us to do alone. But first we must join with Jesus. Only then can the little magnet use the strength of the big magnet.

See, now they are touching one another. The little one can do much more. It holds all my paperclips. The little magnet says, "I can do all things in Him who strengthens me." How true that is for us when Jesus becomes our Savior.

17

Take a Chance

Interest Object: A Monopoly board with chance cards.

Main Truth: Choose Jesus for a chance at eternal life.

Scripture Text: "He who has the Son has life; he who has not the Son has not life" (1 John 5:12).

People all over the world enjoy playing Monopoly. The object of this game is to make lots of money from the bank or from the other players. The winner is whoever winds up with all of the money while the losers go broke.

The game becomes very exciting when we roll the dice and move around the board. Carefully now. Don't land on property which belongs to someone else. You might have to pay high rent. Better to land on your own property.

Do you know what I dread most? Sooner or later every player lands on a chance square. When that happens to me, then I must take a chance. Some chance cards bring very bad luck. "Go to jail! Do not pass go and do not collect $200." Or "Go to the nearest utility, roll dice and pay owner ten times the value."

Whenever I land on a chance square and find myself forced to take a chance, I have a secret wish. I wish that someone would take out all of the bad risks from this stack of chance cards. They could leave all the good chances which would then cause me no fear. How fun to read "Every player must pay you $100!"

Yes, Monopoly is much like life. We would rather have choice without chance. No risks. Let's avoid any chance of something bad.

But you cannot always avoid bad things. Sometimes something bad happens to you. Maybe you get sick. Or your best friend moves away leaving you lonely. Or you may have an automobile accident and get hurt!

This may sound like life is just a series of aimless chances, but wait! In the most important decision of eternity, you need not leave anything to chance. You have a choice about heaven, hell, death, and life.

Jesus is the Son of God and the Savior of all who trust Him. If you accept Him into your life, then death is not bad. You can have eternal life with Jesus.

Sooner or later each one of us must choose. I pray that you will make your choice on the chance of a lifetime. There is no risk in Jesus. "He who has the son has life; he who has not the son of God has not life."

18

Football Fever

Interest Object: A football.

Main Truth: Jesus is our coach who gives us instructions for life.

Scripture Text: "I can do nothing on my own authority; as I hear, I judge; and my judgment is just, because I seek not my own will but the will of him who sent me" (John 5:30).

Any time is a good time for our favorite sport of football. We enjoy watching these athletes push, bump, and struggle on the scrimmage line. It looks confusing, but the basic goal is simple. They try to run, throw, or kick the ball past their opponents for points.

On the playing field a quarterback is the man in charge. Do you ever wonder what goes on in the quarterback huddle before every play? The quarterback chooses the next play and tells his players the secret number in his chant which will start the ball moving. He gives orders and instructions. Every teammate must understand the next play and be ready to do his own job.

Then the players all line up for action. Some teammates try to block their opponents so running-backs can carry the ball through the open space in the line. Or they may protect the quarterback so he can have time to throw the ball. How exciting when a player called the receiver slips into the end zone and catches the ball for a touchdown!

The quarterback is a hero for choosing the right play and making a good throw. He is the boss who runs the team there on the field.

But wait. Who is the fellow standing on the sideline with a clipboard in his hand? He points to the bench and new players enter the game as replacements. He looks very important.

Then we notice the quarterback always looks over his shoulder toward this friend on the sideline. They know each other very well. It turns out that this man is the coach and the quarterback's boss. The quarterback was simply picking plays previously planned by the coach.

No wonder the quarterback keeps looking toward his coach. He wants to be sure the real boss is pleased. If a change is needed, the coach will signal or call directions for the quarterback to relay to the team.

The coach of a football team reminds us of Jesus. I may think I am my own boss, but all through life Jesus is nearby giving encouragement and instruction. "I can do nothing on my own authority." "I seek not my own will but the will of Him who sent me."

That is how Jesus explained His actions while on

earth. He did everything the Father wanted Him to do. Now we must do everything Jesus wants us to do. He is our leader.

19

In God We Trust

Interest Object: A handful of coins.

Main Truth: We can always trust God.

Scripture Text: "Trust in the Lord with all your heart, and do not rely on your own insight. In all your ways acknowledge him, and he will make straight your paths" (Prov. 3:5–6).

Listen to these familiar sounds as I shake something together in my hand. You recognize the sound of coins jingling in a pocket or a hand. Let's pretend we are planning a party with these coins.

As we begin our plans, I need to know something. Do you trust me? Good. Even though we are pretending, it is important that you believe me. So here is my plan.

You can take this money to the store across the street and buy some cookies for our party. But before I give you this money, I need to know something. "Can I trust you?"

After you have convinced me to trust you with my money, I will send you on your way. Don't forget to stop and look both ways before you cross the street. Sometimes a car will stop in the middle of the street with the driver signaling you that it is safe to cross. You look at him and understand what he means. But can you trust him? Surely he would not stop and then try to run over you.

After finally getting across the street and into the store, you choose a package of cookies. The brand name is on the label. Other writing offers a list of ingredients and tells how much the package weighs. Can you trust the label? Certain laws require the truth in packaging.

Finally you take the cookies to the check-out stand. The cashier rings the sale and takes the money. Now it is her time to wonder, "Can I trust that this money is not counterfeit?"

Well, by now you understand my point. In life we must do a lot of trusting. Sometimes people let us down, so we won't trust them anymore. But there is one place in life where our trust will never be disappointed.

Look at these coins. Each one says "In God We Trust." That is a wonderful truth. The Bible teaches us to trust in the Lord. Not just a little but a lot. "Trust in the Lord with all your heart."

20

Grow in Our Lord

Interest Object: A yardstick.

Main Truth: Our best growth is growing in our Lord.

Scripture Text: "But grow in the grace and knowledge of our Lord and Savior Jesus Christ" (2 Peter 3:18).

Boys and girls are always growing. And that is good. You would not want to be a baby or little child all your life! So how many ways can you describe or measure growth?

A good place to start is with this yardstick. You know how. You back up to a wall and place the ruler on the top of your head. No fair standing on tiptoes! Then you move over and use the yardstick to measure your height from the floor to the mark.

Another method to measure growth is by weight in pounds. Climb on the scales and count the pounds. You probably weigh more now than just a few months ago.

The calendar is yet another popular means to describe growth by months or years. Surely you would not forget your birthday! You have probably marked your birthday on a calendar at home. Because a birthday usually means presents and maybe even a party, you are excited when the calendar shows that your birthday is soon.

Now don't overlook one of the most obvious signs of all when your clothes or shoes are no longer the right size. Boys and girls love to outgrow their clothes. When your pants become too short or too tight, then you know you have been growing.

These are different ways to measure physical growth of your body, but surely you have been changing more than just in body. What about your spiritual improvement? Every time you memorize a Bible verse or understand something new about Jesus, you "grow in the grace and knowledge of our Lord and Savior Jesus Christ."

That is what Peter told us to do. No matter how old or smart or big we become, we must all continue to grow spiritually. Every day we can learn more about Jesus. Our love and devotion to Him increases.

21

Good Habits

Interest Object: Tooth brush.

Main Truth: Good habits have good reasons to be continued.

Scripture Text: "Let us consider how to stir up one another to love and good works, not neglecting to meet together as is the habit of some . . ." (Heb. 10:24–25).

Let's be serious now. Do you have any habits? With everyone watching will you admit to any habits?

Children are usually more honest than adults. A pastor asked a group these questions and waited. Everyone tried to avoid looking at the pastor because they feared he would call them by name. Finally one lady laughed nervously and said, "Now, pastor, I'm not going to confess any of my bad habits in public. You already know them anyway!"

Wait a minute. Who said anything about *bad* habits?

Everyone just assumes that all habits are bad, but some habits are good.

Let's think in the positive. Everyone has habits. We are creatures of habits—some good and some bad. Eating good food is a good habit. So is brushing your teeth after meals.

Parents often remind you, "Don't forget to brush your teeth." Then say it so often that children sometimes complain: "When I grow up I'm never going to brush my teeth!"

Now that's foolish. When those children grow up and leave home, they always brush their teeth. You know why? They realize that this is a very good habit for clean breath and healthy teeth. Their parents had good reason to remind them.

However, some adults are so strange. We occasionally hear someone say, "When I was a child my parents made me go to church. I always said that when I grow up, I'll never go back. I'm grown now, so no one can make me go."

Now isn't that silly? They act like going to church is terrible. It's not. The Bible tells us to attend church, "not neglecting to meet together, as is the habit of some, but encouraging one another, and all the more as you see the Day drawing near" (Heb. 10:25).

Going to church every week is a good habit like brushing your teeth regularly. You don't hear adults saying, "When I was a child my parents made me brush my teeth, but now I'm grown. I'll never do it again!"

Good habits have good reasons to be continued. Going to church is a good habit.

22

Cover Up or Clean Up

Interest Object: Can of air freshener.

Main Truth: Don't cover up sin. Confess your sins to God who can clean you.

Scripture Text: "I finally admitted all my sins to you and stopped trying to hide them. I said to myself, 'I will confess them to the Lord.' And you forgave me. All my guilt is gone" (Ps. 32:5 LB).

Here is a can filled with a pleasant fragrance. I'll spray it into the air for you to smell while I tell you this story.

Children in a school class entered one day to see their teacher spraying the classroom with a can like this. After a while the can was empty. Then everyone began to smell something very bad. Evidently a rat had hidden in the room and died. The odor was terrible.

Then the teacher got very nervous. She sent students

throughout the school borrowing cans of air freshener from other teachers. Before noon all the cans were gone and the bad odor was worse.

Finally, one of her students made a very good suggestion. "Teacher, why don't we just find the dead rat and get rid of it?"

Good idea! Instead of covering up, they would clean up. And they did. One of the boys found the rat and removed it. Then everyone could breathe again.

That's how we must deal with our sins. Whenever we do wrong we feel bad inside. It's like having something dead in your pocket. You can't just ignore it or pretend that nothing is wrong. That's a cover-up. You need to clean up.

The Bible teaches us that we must admit or confess to God our wrongs. Then they won't be hidden. God takes them far away and leaves us clean.

King David learned this lesson. Listen to how he explained it. "I finally admitted all my sins to you and stopped trying to hide them. I said to myself, 'I will confess them to the Lord.' And you forgave me! All my guilt is gone."

23

A Happy Face

Interest Object: Picture of smiling clown or a real clown in person.

Main Truth: For a happy face on the outside we need the joy of Jesus inside.

Scripture Text: "These things I have spoken to you, that my joy may be in you, and that your joy may be full" (John 15:11).

Everyone loves a clown because he smiles and helps make us happy. When we are happy we feel better. Sometimes a doctor will invite a clown to a hospital to cheer up the children. The doctor knows that a merry heart does good like a medicine.

But what happens when the clown himself doesn't feel very happy? Perhaps he is tired or sad. Well, a popular song tells us to "Put On a Happy Face." That is exactly what the clown does. When he puts on his clown makeup, he usually paints a big, happy smile on his face.

What is fine for a clown won't really help us, however. We can't wear a mask or a false smile painted on our faces.

Jesus talked about happiness and joy. He taught us that the best way to look happy on the outside is to have the joy of Jesus inside. When we think of how wonderful He is, then we become happy. We can smile.

Jesus said, "These things I have spoken to you, that my joy may be in you, and that your joy may be full" (John 15:11). The joy of Jesus fills us all the way from our hearts to our faces.

For an experiment today, let's remember how much Jesus loves us. With that thought we can all smile.

As you return to your seats take the smile with you. In the congregation today there may be some people who are not very happy. They need joy inside. Your smile can remind them that Jesus loves everyone.

24

How Far Will a Dollar Go?

Interest Object: A silver dollar.

Main Truth: We can fulfill Jesus' command by giving to missions.

Scripture Text: "And he said to them, 'Go into all the world and preach the gospel to the whole creation'" (Mark 16:15).

There's an old story about George Washington, our first president, throwing a silver dollar like this one, across the Potomac River in Virginia. Well, I don't know if any of you have ever seen the Potomac River, but it's so wide there's almost no way anybody could ever throw a silver dollar across it, even George Washington.

But would you believe I can make this dollar go all the way around the world? [They will undoubtedly answer "no!"] I can! Not by throwing it, but by putting it in this envelope marked "Mission Offering." Then, I put the

59

envelope in the offering plate. It's counted, then deposited in the bank in the church's account, along with everyone else's gifts to missions.

Then the church sends a check to our missions board and from there they send some money to South America to build churches, to Europe to train preachers, to Africa to feed starving people, to the Middle East to preach good news, and to the Orient to buy Bibles. And it goes to many other places to help in other ways. A part of every dollar I give in church reaches many people and places.

So I can make a dollar go all the way around the world. But not if I toss it. And not if I keep it. Only if I give it.

Jesus said, "Go into all the world and preach the gospel" (Mark 16:15). One way we can do this is by giving our money. We can fulfill Jesus' command by giving money to missions. And also our prayers for missions can go around the world.

Why don't you see how much you can give this year? Your dollars will go all around the world!

25

Unlocking God's Promises

Interest Object: A padlock with a key.

Main Truth: Patient faith is the key to God's promises.

Scripture Text: "We do not want you to become lazy, but to imitate those who through faith and patience inherit what has been promised" (Heb. 6:12, NIV).

To promise means to give your word. You have to keep a promise, be true to your word. A promise is like putting a lock on your word.

You know how this lock works. You put this part through something you want to lock up, then snap the lock closed. To open the lock you need a key, or sometimes a combination. Here's the key for this lock. Put it in here, turn it, the lock opens.

God has made lots of promises. He has kept them all. Some He is still keeping. He promises to supply all our needs, answer our prayers, forgive us when we sin, give us eternal life.

How do we claim these promises of God? Is there a key or combination to enable us to unlock God's promises?

Just as there is a key for this lock, patient faith is the key to God's promises. Have faith in God that He will keep His word. And be patient. Sometimes we have to wait on the Lord. But He always rewards patient faith and keeps His promises.

Hebrews 6:12 says, ". . . imitate those who through faith and patience inherit what has been promised." God will keep His word if we will patiently believe.

26

Why Go to Church?

Interest Object: A large feather.

Main Truth: We should go to church to encourage others and be encouraged ourselves.

Scripture Text: "Let us not give up meeting together, as some are in the habit of doing, but let us encourage one another" (Heb. 10:25, NIV).

Look at this beautiful feather! It is so soft and light and colorful. [Stroke it with the grain of the feather.] But watch what happens when I stroke the feather the opposite way. [Stroke against the grain.] It becomes all ruffled and separated and doesn't look as pretty. If I stroke it the right way, it's nice. [Stroke it with the grain to restore it.] And if I stroke it the wrong way, it's yucky.

This feather has something to teach us about the church. The church has a purpose. It is to be a place of love and encouragement to people. When we are together, fulfilling our purpose, we are pleasing God and helping each other. Like the feather when you rub it the right way, the church looks beautiful to God.

But if we get out of the habit of going to church, it's like rubbing the feather the wrong way. The church can't fulfill its purpose if people don't attend, and it becomes ruffled and separated. So, we should go to church to encourage others and be encouraged ourselves. Then God's church fulfills its purpose.

Let's hear and obey the words of Hebrews 10:25, "Let us not give up meeting together, as some are in the habit of doing, but let us encourage one another."

27

How Christ Changes Us

Interest Object: A few pieces of uncooked spaghetti and a small dish of cooked spaghetti without sauce.

Main Truth: When we believe in Christ He changes us by making us new inside.

Scripture Text: "Therefore, if anyone is in Christ, he is a new creation; the old has passed away, behold, the new has come" (2 Cor. 5:17).

One of my favorite things to eat is spaghetti. Here is some uncooked spaghetti. It is hard and brittle. It breaks easily. And it doesn't taste like cooked spaghetti.

Now here's some cooked spaghetti. It is soft and tasty. Yum! Cooking this hard, brittle spaghetti in boiling salted water changed it into something delicious. It is still spaghetti. It is still made of the same ingredients.

It has just been changed so it is much more edible and enjoyable.

Boys and girls, when we believe in Christ He changes us by making us new inside. He takes away our sin by forgiving us. He puts His Holy Spirit in us to guide us. We may still look the same on the outside, but Christ changes us inwardly and we are reborn through Him. We are still made the same way, but now we are remade by Christ. Like the spaghetti—same but changed. Jesus Christ changes us within when we come to Him in faith.

This illustrates what the apostle Paul meant when he wrote in 2 Corinthians 5:17, "Therefore if anyone is in Christ, he is a new creation; the old has passed away, behold, the new has come."

Let Jesus into your life by believing He is God and can take away your sin through His life, death, and resurrection. You can be a changed person!

28

Sunday Is Special

Interest Object: You could use a number of things to communicate the truth of this text. You could substitute marbles, colored eggs, even cut circles from different colors of construction paper. I used tennis balls, six of one color and one of a different color. The principle is the same whatever you choose to use.

Main Truth: Sunday is the Christian's special day to worship and rest.

Scripture Text: "Remember the sabbath day, to keep it holy" (Exod. 20:8).

I have seven tennis balls here. They are all the same—round, rubber inside, coated by fuzzy stuff. They all bounce. Each has the same purpose, to play tennis.

But one of the seven tennis balls is a different color. It's my favorite. It's the only one I have of this color. I think I play better using this ball than I do with the others. It's special to me.

God gave us seven days in a week. Each has twenty-four hours in it. Things have to be done each day. One day is pretty much like all the others.

Except one. Sunday. Sunday is different. Sunday is the Lord's Day. On Sunday we put on nice clothes and go to Sunday school and church instead of school or work. Why? What's so special about Sunday?

Well, a long time ago, God gave His people Ten Commandments. The fourth commandment says, "Remember the sabbath day, to keep it holy." It was the seventh day and God said it was to be especially His day. No work. Only rest and worship.

For a long time God's people rested and worshiped on Saturday, the Sabbath. Then, after Jesus rose on a Sunday, Christians changed from Saturday to Sunday as the day for rest and worship. On Sunday we celebrate Jesus' resurrection, remember God in worship, and rest from work or school.

Sunday is special. It must always be. We remember God and He recreates us, refreshes us.

Make Sunday a special day in your week, every week. Sunday is the Christian's special day for worship and rest.

29

The Way to God

Interest Object: A plate of paper cookies. Cut them out of cardboard or construction paper. Or ball up small bits of paper to look like cookies. They don't have to look too real.

Main Truth: Believing in Jesus Christ is the only way to get to God.

Scripture Text: "Jesus said to him, 'I am the way, and the truth, and the life; no one comes to the Father, but by me'" (John 14:6).

I like cookies! So today I brought a plate of cookies to share with you [pass around plate of fake cookies].

There is only one problem. These cookies are paper! They are not the real thing. We would get awfully hungry if all we had to eat were paper cookies.

Now let's apply this to religion. A lot of religious people will tell you many ways to get to God and heaven. They will say, "Be good," or "join the church," or "give money," or "read the Bible and learn how to pray."

But there's only one way to get to God. Believing in Jesus Christ is the only way to get to God. Jesus said in John 14:6, "I am the way, and the truth, and the life; no one comes to the Father, but by me."

Believing in Jesus Christ is the only way to get to God and heaven. Jesus is the real thing—the way, truth and life. You can trust Him. He will get you to God!

30

God Wants Our Best

Interest Object: A poster promoting some church activity. One side of the poster should be neat and attractive. The reverse side should be messy, with crooked letters, a misspelled word, blobs of ink, and some bad smudges.

Main Truth: God wants our best in everything we do.

Scripture Text: "Whatever you do, do well" (Eccles. 9:10a, LB).

There are two ways to do anything. We can do the best we can, or we can do less than our best. Which does God want?

I thought about that as I was making this poster about Vacation Bible School. You can see how sloppy and yucky I did it the first time I tried [show bad side]. I even misspelled this word. Well, I just wasn't satisfied with it.

So I decided to try again and do the very best I could. Here is the result [turn poster over to good side]. This may not be as good as someone else could do it, but it's the best I can do, so I am satisfied with it.

That's what God asks of each of us. Our best. Ecclesiastes 9:10 says, in the Living Bible's paraphrase, "Whatever you do, do well." God wants our best in everything we do. At home, school, church, work, always do your best. That's the only way you will ever be satisfied with the things you do. And it pleases God for us to give our best. God wants our best. Let's do our best to please Him.

31

The Thing You Can't Tame

Interest Object: An imaginary pet flea.

Main Truth: Though we can never fully control what we say, we must never stop trying.

Scripture Text: "All kinds of animals, birds, reptiles and creatures of the sea are being tamed and have been tamed by man, but no man can tame the tongue" (James 3:7–8a, NIV).

I want to talk to you today about the thing you can't tame. I'll do it by talking about something you can tame. [Reach into pocket, pretending to take out something tiny and put it onto open palm of hand.]

This is Freddie, my pet flea. I got him off the ear of a dog, and I've trained him to do tricks.

Freddie, stand on your head [tilt your head sideways as if he were doing it].

Freddie, roll over [move your head in a circle like you are watching him roll over].

Good, Freddie. Now, do a back flip [snap head up sharply]. No, no, Freddie, I said back flip. That was a front flip. Do a back flip [snap head again]. That's it! Sometimes Freddie doesn't mind.

Now, Freddie, do a double back flip [rotate head in circle twice].

Wasn't Freddie great? Let's all give him a big hand! [Clap, pretending to mash Freddie, who is still in your hand, in the process.]

Oh, no, I smashed Freddie [wipe hand on clothes]. Oh, well, I'll get another flea and train him, because any animal can be trained. Lions, tigers, elephants, whales, even fleas can be tamed.

But there's one thing that can't be tamed. James 3:7–8 tells us about it. "All kinds of animals, birds, reptiles and creatures of the sea are being tamed and have been tamed by men, but no man can tame the tongue." That means we can never fully control what we say. But does that mean we shouldn't care about what we say? Of course not!

Though we can never fully control what we say, we must never stop trying. What we say does matter. We must keep on caring about what we say and how we say it.

32

Walking in Love

Interest Object: A pair of Indian moccasins or a picture of moccasins.

Main Truth: We must walk in love.

Scripture Text: "If your brother is being injured by what you eat, you are no longer walking in love" (Rom. 14:15).

There's an old Indian saying, "Let me not criticize my brother until I have walked two miles in his moccasins." These are moccasins. They're the Indian's shoes. And criticize means to look down on or talk ugly about.

The saying means don't talk ugly about someone, because we never know their life and all about them. We can't walk in someone else's shoes, can't put our lives into theirs. But we can walk in love for all people.

How do we walk in love? Try to understand others.

Don't judge them or be critical of them. Be kind to others. Put others first. That's not only the Indian way, that's also Jesus' way!

Romans 14:15 says, "If your brother is being injured by what you eat, you are no longer walking in love." This means if we do anything to hurt others, we are not showing them Jesus' love.

Let's walk in love so others will know we love Jesus and come to love Him too.

33

Getting Along with Others

Main Truth: To get along with others we must act "medium."

Scripture Text: "Let your moderation be known unto all men" (Phil. 4:5, KJV).

I want to talk to you today about getting along with others. This is important. In school, on the playground, when meeting new people, it's important as Christians to get along with other people. *All* other people.

The secret of getting along with others is found in Philippians 4:5. "Let your moderation be known unto all men." Let me tell you a story I heard that helps us understand what this verse means and how to get along with people.

Some little boys were building a clubhouse. They gathered scraps of wood and hunks of cardboard. When they finished it they decided they needed some rules for the club. So they thought and thought and came up with three rules. They were:

1. Nobody act big.
2. Nobody act small.
3. Everybody act medium.

I like that! It's the same thing Paul said in Philippians 4:5, "Let your moderation be known unto all men." That means, "everybody act medium." To get along with others we must act "medium."

Nobody act big, like you're better than anybody else, or smarter, or richer. Don't be pushy or a bully.

Nobody act small, because you're no worse than anybody else. God made you and that's good. You don't ever need to feel like you're not as good as others. Don't act small.

Act medium. Be yourself. Don't go overboard on anything. Be honest and real. Act like Jesus! Then you will get along with others, you will be happy and God will be pleased.

34

Getting Around to It

Interest Object: A circle cut from colored paper with TUIT written on it. Make a circle with TUIT written on it for each child.

Main Truth: We should use our time wisely, not putting things off.

Scripture Text: "Look carefully then how you walk, not as unwise men but as wise, making the most of the time, because the days are evil" (Eph. 5:15–16).

Do you like to put things off? There are some things I just don't like to do, so I put them off as long as possible. Like going to the dentist. Or doing my income tax. I say to myself, "Well, when I get around to it, I'll do that."

I'll bet you could think of some things you put off, like cleaning your room, or yardwork, or homework. You say, "When I get around to it, I'll do it."

Some people even put off big decisions in life, like getting married or accepting Jesus. Some people never get around to it.

So, since we all put things off until we get around to it, I made some "round TUITS" for us. See? It's round. And it says "TUIT" on it. Now, you have an "around to it" and don't have to put things off anymore!

That's silly, isn't it? But the point is, we ought not to make excuses and put things off that ought to be done. That's just as silly. We should use our time wisely, not putting things off.

There's even a verse of Scripture that tells us so. It's Ephesians 5:15–16, and it says, "Look carefully then how you walk, not as unwise men but as wise, making the most of the time, because the days are evil."

35

Getting Attention

Interest Object: A loud whistle.

Main Truth: God watches over us all the time to supply every need we have.

Scripture Text: "The Lord is my shepherd, I shall not want" (Ps. 23:1).

I have a problem sometimes at my house. The problem is how to get the attention I need. We all need recognition and attention. Sometimes I don't get enough.

So, I've tried to figure out ways to get more attention. Maybe I could just be real loud, you know, talk loudly and bang things around. Or maybe I could do something to call attention to myself—like stand on my head. That would get attention!

How about this whistle? I could call it my attention-getting whistle. Every time I felt neglected, I could get attention by blowing on the whistle. Then the rest of the family would know my needs, stop what they're doing and give me some attention. Is that a good way?

Can you think of a better way? How about being kind, doing something helpful, being loving or thoughtful? Or maybe when we feel neglected we can just say so and ask for a little attention. Say, "Hey, I need a little of your time and attention."

How do we get God's attention? The good news is, we don't have to! We have it! All the time! God watches over us all the time to supply every need we have. Even the need of recognition or attention.

Psalm 23:1 says, "The Lord is my shepherd; I shall not want." This means God watches over us like a shepherd cares for his sheep. All our needs are met. God cares for us!

36

God's Beautiful World

Interest Object: A globe of the world.

Main Truth: The beauty of God's world is all around us if we'll just look at it.

Scripture Text: "The heavens are telling the glory of God; and the firmament proclaims his handiwork" (Ps. 19:1).

Have you ever stopped to think about how beautiful God's world is? The beauty of God's world is all around us if we will just look for it.

This is a globe, a miniature model of the planet Earth. God made the Earth, and all the other planets and the universe they're in. Even this globe is beautiful, with its different colors of blue for the ocean, greens and yellows and purples for the lands. God made color too. He must like blues and greens, because He created so much of those colors.

I think God put us here on earth to enjoy all He created. We must help take care of God's creation. And we should praise God for all the beauty He created. Hundreds of years ago, King David of Israel did just that. He looked at God's creation and wrote a psalm of praise. David exclaimed, "The heavens are telling the glory of God; and the firmament proclaims his handiwork."

This week as you look at the blue sky, white clouds, green grass and trees, brightly colored clothes, colors of people's skin, remember that God made those things for us to enjoy. Give thanks and praise to God for the beautiful world He made. And enjoy it!

37

Experiencing God's Love

Interest Object: A jar full of candy.

Main Truth: We each need a personal experience of God's love through faith.

Scripture Text: "For God so loved the world, that he gave his only begotten Son, that whosoever believeth in him should not perish, but have everlasting life" (John 3:16, KJV).

I love to eat candy! So today I brought my candy jar with me. It happens to have my favorite kind of candy in it—cherry balls. Now I want you to know how good these cherry balls are. So I'll describe them to you.

They're red, and round. Here, I'll unwrap one. It's kind of sticky feeling, and hard. I'll put it into my mouth. Yum, it's good! Tastes like cherry. Real sweet.

Kind of sticky at first, but now it's real smooth and slick. It sure is delicious!

Now, you know how good these cherry balls are, right? No? Well, I told you! How could you know better how they really are? Oh, if you ate one for yourself? Okay, pass the jar around and each person take one.

Boys and girls, experiencing God is much like experiencing the candy. We each need a personal experience of God's love through faith. We don't really know God personally just by hearing somebody tell about him. Watching others who know God doesn't give us a personal experience with Him. How can we experience God's love?

The only way you can personally experience God's love is to believe in Him yourself. You must invite Him into your life and say directly to Him, "Lord, I believe." I can't do it for you. Neither can your mom or dad or anyone else.

It says in John 3:16, "For God so loved the world, that he gave his only begotten Son, that whosoever believeth in him should not perish, but have everlasting life."

38

Trusting God's Strength

Interest Objects: A small pitcher of water, a large bowl, a
  tissue, and a paper cup for each child.

Main Truth: God has strength we can trust in when our
  own fails.

Scripture Text: "Trust ye in the Lord forever: for in the
  Lord Jehovah is everlasting strength" (Isa. 26:4, KJV).

I'm thirsty. Excuse me please while I pour myself a drink. Let's see, here's a pitcher of water. I need
something to pour it into. Oh, here's a tissue. [Circle
your fingers and thumb into a cup shape and put the tissue down into it. Hold hand over large bowl or you'll
have a mess.] I'll pour myself a drink into this tissue.

Oops, it won't hold water! Maybe there's something
else. Oh, yes, here's a paper cup [pour water, drink].

Now let's see, the tissue wouldn't hold the water but
the cup would. They are both paper. The difference is,

one is strengthened with wax and the other isn't.

There will be times in your life when trouble flows like water. Without faith in God you will be like the tissue, unable to withstand the trouble. But with faith in God, you will be like the cup, strengthened for the task.

Our human strength isn't enough to withstand life's problems. God has strength we can trust when our own fails. He will strengthen us if we trust Him.

Isaiah said, "Trust ye in the Lord forever: for in the Lord Jehovah is everlasting strength."

39

Aids to Remembering

Interest Object: A piece of bright ribbon tied on the pastor's finger and a piece of ribbon for each child.

Main Truth: The Lord's Supper helps us remember who Jesus was and what He did for us.

Scripture Text: "This is my body which is for you. Do this in remembrance of me. . . . This cup is the new covenant in my blood. Do this, as often as your drink it, in remembrance of me" (1 Cor. 11:24–25).

D o you ever forget things? I do! All the time. So I use a little gimmick to help me remember things. Like this piece of ribbon I tied on my finger to remind me to come to church today. A lot of people tie string on their fingers as an aid to remembering, or write notes to themselves, or do a lot of other things so they won't be so forgetful.

The human mind is limited, so we sometimes use different aids to help us remember things.

I think God knew people would be forgetful. So He gave us an aid to remember the most important thing He ever did for us.

The most important thing? Jesus! He came and lived and died and rose again, that by faith we can have eternal life. God doesn't want us to forget that, so He gave us a beautiful aid for remembering. We call it communion or Lord's Supper.

Jesus said, "This is my body which is for you. Do this in remembrance of me. This is the new covenant in my blood. Do this, as often as you drink it, in remembrance of me." He was speaking of the bread and cup we use in communion. They are reminders of Jesus—who He was, what He did. Let them remind us of Him today as we come to the Lord's table. If you are His, all of this is yours!

40

The Best Christmas Gift

Interest Object: A large hand mirror.

Main Truth: God gave us Jesus and wants us to give ourselves to Him.

Scripture Text: "And going into the house they saw the child with Mary his mother, and they fell down and worshiped him. Then, opening their treasures, they offered him gifts, gold and frankincense and myrrh" (Matt. 2:11).

The thing I enjoy most about Christmas is giving gifts. I like to give the best gifts I can afford to those I love.

Christmas has always been a time for giving. On the first Christmas, when Jesus was born, wise men visited Him. They gave Him gifts of gold and frankincense and myrrh. Since that time people have exchanged gifts at Christmastime.

But while it's nice to give Christmas gifts to each other, it would be better to give something to Jesus. What would He want from us? Money for missions? A promise to attend Sunday school and church every Sunday? But these are small things.

I can show you what Jesus really wants for Christmas. [Hold up mirror and turn it so each child can see himself in it.]

No, he doesn't want a mirror! What did you see *in* the mirror? Yourself! God gave us Jesus and He wants us to give ourselves to Jesus.

41

Who Do You Trust?

Interest Object: A volunteer to demonstrate trust.

Main Truth: God never lets us down when we trust in Him.

Scripture Text: "Trust in the Lord with all your heart, and lean not on your own understanding; in all your ways acknowledge Him, and He shall direct your paths" (Prov. 3:5–6, NKJV).

I want to show you what trust is. Brian, will you come up here and help me, please? Now, Brian, do you trust me? Are you sure? Okay, then put your hands on your hips and turn your back to me.

Okay, Brian, keep your legs straight, don't move your feet, and fall backwards. I will catch you. [This may take a couple of tries. Trust is easier to say than do. If you try it two or three times and the child still doesn't cooperate fully, just make a point of his not trusting fully but we can still trust God fully. Otherwise, as follows.]

We saw that Brian didn't really trust me the first time. But then he knew I'd catch him, so he did as I said the second time. From this we learn that trust is believing in someone, relying on them and being able to give yourself to them.

Who do you trust? People? Well, sometimes you can trust some people. Money? We can trust in money. But money can leave us easily, leaving nothing to trust. Notice, on the money it says, "In God We Trust."

We can trust God! Always! For anything and everything. God never lets us down.

Proverbs 3:5–6 says, "Trust in the Lord with all your heart, and lean not on your own understanding; in all your ways acknowledge Him, and He shall direct your paths."

42

The Greatest Thing that Ever Happened

Interest Object: A bookmark for each child. Religious bookstores often have a good selection. One depicting the resurrection would be most appropriate.

Main Truth: Jesus' resurrection is the greatest thing that ever happened.

Scripture Text: "But the angel said to the women, 'Do not be afraid; for I know that you seek Jesus who was crucified. He is not here; for he has risen, as he said. Come, see the place where he lay'" (Matt. 28:5–6).

Whathat do you think is the greatest thing that ever happened? Some of you might say it was when Christopher Columbus discovered America. Others would say it was the first man on the moon. Or maybe you've seen the space shuttle take off and think that's the greatest. No doubt some of you would say the day

95

you were born is the greatest thing that ever happened.

Let me tell you what I think the greatest thing is. I think it's the resurrection of Jesus! Without Jesus' resurrection we wouldn't have Christianity, or any real hope for eternal life. When Jesus rose from the grave He guaranteed that all He said and did was true.

Each of the four gospels—Matthew, Mark, Luke, and John—tell about the resurrection. I want you to go home, get your Bible and read about it. Then, take one of these bookmarks and put it in the place where it tells about Jesus' resurrection. Mark it well. Underline it. It's the greatest thing that ever happened!